Waving Mustard in Surrender

Also by Al Ortolani

Slow Stirring Spoon (chapbook), High/Coo Press, 1981
The Last Hippie of Camp 50, Woodley Press, 1989
Finding the Edge, Woodley Press, 2011
Wren's House, Coal City Press, 2012
Cooking Chili on the Day of the Dead, Aldrich Press, 2013 ⸱

Waving Mustard in Surrender

poems by

Al Ortolani

NYQ Books™

The New York Quarterly Foundation, Inc.
New York, New York

NYQ Books™ is an imprint of The New York Quarterly Foundation, Inc.

The New York Quarterly Foundation, Inc.
P. O. Box 2015
Old Chelsea Station
New York, NY 10113

www.nyq.org

First Edition

Set in New Baskerville

Layout by Raymond P. Hammond
Cover Design by Christina Sinibaldi

Cover Illustration: "Surrender" by Jacque Forsher | www.jacqueforsher.com

Library of Congress Control Number: 2014915666

ISBN: 978-1-935520-99-3

For

Karissa Ortolani Reeves, Blane Reeves,
Theresa Ortolani Middleton, Wes Middleton,
Tyler Allen, Staci Allen

Contents

III. Bucket and Broom

IV. New Start in a Meat Wrapper

Acknowledgements, Notes, Thank You, About the Author

I. Cussing Bill Mazeroski

Kisser

No time for self-pity
on a baseball diamond
with so many dusty
ground balls short-hopping
the infield. Sometimes
you have little more
to respond to than
a quick crack of the
bat. If for even
a second, you take
your eye off the ball,
you're flattened, the
hot shot smacking
you in the kisser,
and then, there you are
lying on your back,
alone between second
and third, adrenaline
pumping, the other
dug out cheering.
You remember Tony Kubek,
downed by a pebble,
being carried from the
field in Pittsburgh,
the fifth grade boys
crying into their gloves,
cussing Bill Mazeroski
when he kissed
the ball in the ninth.

Suicide Squeeze

You've been trained to bunt,
to sacrifice to either baseline.
At third, your teammate
has decoded the pitcher's
move from the mound.
He has identified the flexed knee,
the arm angle
of no return. All movement
is committed
to a single collision.
You square your shoulders,
sliding your knuckles to
the trademark. You have
no choice with the squeeze on,
but to stay loose on the shaft
and to see the ball
to the barrel of the bat.
The lights are bright.
Beer and peanuts are for sale.

Soaring Fins

We found Uncle Bobby
drunk again on 8th Street, curled
around the base of a tired forsythia
like a berm of topsoil.

Mother said load him
into the back of the station wagon
before the neighbors wake,
careful not to bang his head
on nothing sharp. Dad said
best leave him where he lay
he made good as compost.

Then he chewed his cigar
and studied the opposite curb
as my brothers folded
Bobby's legs through
the ultra-wide electric window,
which in the '59 Plymouth
looked out backwards
on the zinc smelters, Chubb's Bar,
the promise of soaring fins.

Brothers

We live in a truck
that hasn't been seized
by the bank. Dad
keeps it hidden under
the name of his brother.
We sleep on mattresses
made from cushions of
couches. We cook on
a Coleman, picked up
at a garage sale, and
eat cross-legged out
of cans. My brother
tapes up photographs
from *Sports Illustrated*
of Eli and Peyton Manning,
brothers like us. I keep
a photo of mom, her
two boys beside her on Christmas
morning. She sips
coffee and has a bow
on her head. Three mattresses
litter the truck floor.
As soon as the weather
warms, we drive
north for work on
the pipeline. Dad tapes
nothing above his mattress.
He worries about where
to park the truck,
someplace without
police or bums, someplace
with a little light.

Eliot Ness Pisses on Crime

You can pretend like
you are Eliot Ness
ripping the river
with machine gun spray.
All the bad guys in the world
are holding their breath
under water,
waiting in the hope that
you will run out of ammo
before they run out of air.
However, as Eliot Ness,
it's not going to happen.
You have been pissing
from bridges
since time began,
and the bad guys, even
though they dive deeply
are eventually swept
to the surface. It helps
if you're young, stung
with vinegar, untouched
by the shy bladder.

Highway Signs Are Painted Green

On Saturday, Laura left her husband and her boyfriend
       with a symbolic flourish.
She tossed her belongings in a box
and covered them with a tarp.
Not owning much kept it simple. It was no trouble
to slide the box in the trunk of her boyfriend's car and let him drive her
to their usual motel. Neither the boyfriend, nor her husband
      Phil suspected much,

but by midnight after she crushed a Xanax in her boyfriend's beer,
she was thirty miles south on the interstate to Tulsa. A note
on the nightstand consisted of a simple grocery list
in green ink on a motel notepad.

Would you pick these items up at the IGA
and take them to Phil? Tell him
all that you wished I'd said to you. Thank you
for the green blouse you bought from Target.
It matched the color of the eyes I always wished I had.

Hitching by Night across New Mexico

The river of the Milky Way flows
      above the river of the highway.
          Both stream across the desert, stretching
             from horizon to horizon.
                The hitchhiker presses

                     his thumb into a headlight's glare.
          He sucks his knuckle
        like a coyote licking a wound,
     and peers into the open window of a Buick.
The man who drives him to Amarillo
      leans into the steering wheel;

        his hands, thick with turquoise rings,
          fly like wings when he speaks,
             the stub of his cigar
       alive,
      silvered with spit.

Another Tornado Warning

Grandpa puts grandma in the closet with a flashlight,
a bottle of water, and a video poker game.
By and by, he joins her
although he has to sit on a step ladder.
He closes his eyes and listens to Larry
the white cockapoo whimper
below grandma's chair.
As the storm builds, grandpa opens
the closet door. The television casts a pale blue
eye across the living room. Grandma sleeps
and Larry shivers with each roll of thunder.
The St. Louis Cardinals are up by two runs
and Albert Pujols is stepping to the plate.

Playing Mafia Wars on Library Computers

The library computers are available
For one hour per day. I have already
Used my one hour, and have turned in
My numbered, orange time card. Even, though
There are three seats empty and no one
Waiting outside of the door, rules
Are rules. I've hidden behind
The bust of Andrew Carnegie for the shift to change,
For the new library aide to command
The controller's seat, one who doesn't recognize
My black fedora or my shapeless trench coat.

I only need a moment to check my
facebook, to see if any new
Requests from family have found me, not as a fugitive
On the lamb in a library
But as a Don connected to Soldiers.
My Mafia Wars family visits me out of respect,
They kiss my ring and ask for gifts:
Get-away cars, bullet-proof vests and sawed-off shotguns.
Gamers like Fat Freddy, Tony the Guinea,
And Fantasy Hit-Bitch are desperate people.
They have been
Roughed-up by public libraries before.

Spinning Donuts with Grandfather in His Old Ford

He'd take you to the university parking lot
where the snow was laid out
flat and wide like a lake.

Into the swirling flakes he gunned the engine
and sent the truck into a spin.
Cranking hard on the steering wheel,

he sprayed snow in all directions, throwing you
against the far door
and then back in a jumble into

his warm green overcoat,
his great brown mittens
turning the night with ease.

You laughed even when the campus cops
pulled you over,
shaking their heads at the old professor

spinning donuts in the snow.
Do you remember how long it lasted,
gliding in a sideways spin,

the air in the cab,
cold and sparkling, the light
in the ice of your breath?

The Second Generation Visits Vietnam

Somewhere in the hills near Bhak Ma
She sits on a woven mat
With villagers. They search for songs

Common to both cultures.
One is Happy Birthday
And the other Jingle Bells.

They pass cups of wine
And howl at the incongruity
Of their singing.

In the surrounding forests
The night is laden with memory
Both of peach flower and orchid.

She sees this in their eyes
When they sing, when they take
The path to the river, curving

Through, yet detonated, blossoms
Of mortar and claymore.
She wonders in the morning

Will they know her
As they return with buckets of water
Heavy against their shoulders.

Maslow's Hierarchy

Last night Maslow had four hamburgers.
They were smeared in ketchup, mustard
and grilled onions. He cut the grease
with a swallow of light beer
and wiped his hands on his Levi's.

In the back of the bar was this old woman
shooting pool. He'd seen her before.
She aimed her finger at him like it was a pistol
and then blew the smoke away. Maslow
couldn't tell if that was a good sign or not,
so he did the same. She feigned impact,
the finger bullet striking her in the shoulder.
When she flipped onto the pool table felt,
the remaining balls scattered in a solid break.
Her partner helped her up and glared at Maslow
for using a loaded finger in a public place.
This is a family establishment he bellowed
across the room. Maslow shot again.

The imaginary bullet went wide and struck
a *Miller Lite* sign. If the bullet hadn't been imaginary,
the sign would have shattered, sending little shards
of plastic and electricity into the far corners
of the bar. People cleared a path,
barstools clattering to the floor.
The older beauty rechalked her pool cue
and stepped between them. Secretly, she loved
having men fight over her. It hadn't happened
for years, and for a time, she felt sexy
like the deep blue lights
inside of the jukebox. Maslow figured *no blood
no foul,* so he sent the two an order
of amoeba-like sandwiches. The man gave

the woman a knuckle punch
and they racked up the balls like nothing had happened.
Maslow abhorred violence, so he stacked his
empty plate with other empty plates
and holstered his finger, promising
never to wield it again, unless he was called out.

Wild Life in the Big City

Once while jogging down 87th street
I came upon a groundhog that had been
Cornered by a bobcat. At least that
Was my perspective. At first I was concerned
And took it upon myself to intervene
Much like I was breaking up a fight
In the lunchroom. I stepped between them
And forced the groundhog to look me
In the eyes. Assuming that being the smaller
Of the two, he would be inclined
To listen to reason. When I flung my arms
In the air in a shooing motion, he stood
On his hind legs and uttered
A *chit chitchitchit,* a stuttered attack
Upon my philanthropic nature. I was
Indignant at his reproach,
So I turned to the bobcat, and shooed him
With equal fervor. He slouched
Just out of sight beyond the catalpas
And skulked in a primeval pose.
Two days later, I was driving to the Hy-Vee
And the groundhog was standing
Just off the curb in the street, chittering
At an eighteen wheeler, a school bus
And then a cement mixer.
I jerked the steering wheel
Of my Ford Ranger and swerved in a feint
To run him down.
The groundhog stood on his toes
And barred his teeth. In the rear view mirror,
He raised his stubby arm
And flipped me off with his nasty little paw.

Jesus Examines the Blueprints

The wiry little carpenter with the pointed beard
Digs into his tool belt for nails, slips
His pencil behind his ear. He'll work
Sundays if he has too, knowing well
The price of being underbid.
Remodeling costs more per square foot
Than any new spec house
But the old place is a mess. Peter suggests
A triplex. Judas a bulldozer.

As an independent contractor
He's got to start somewhere, if eventually
He wants to turn water into wine
And to divide the fish and the loaves
Among the hungry. Then there's the matter
Of the building permit. The city inspector.
The other guy who walks on water.

T-Ball on the Boulevard

Saturday sun on the guard rail—
a girl of about 8 years plays
t-ball with her grandfather
in the street just to the east
of the Buddhist Center. They use
an orange highway cone for the T.
The bat is scuffed aluminum; the ball
shines white as if new. The girl
is too short to get a level swing,
but with a slight uppercut
the ball sails across the curb
into the weeds beside the I-35
exit ramp. Her grandfather cheers
and raises his arms into the air.
Grandmother in a pink pants suit
fields the ball, chasing it down
in quick, choppy steps
like a left fielder testing
the warning track.

The Velvet Revolution Reaches Kansas

for Henrik Christensen

Otto lived in a house boat on the Neosho River.
Some said he was a pot farmer in hiding. Mostly,
he drank cases of Pilsner, and floated
the corked bottles on limb lines.
On cold nights a foggy light frosted his window;
blue smoke twisted free from the stove chimney.
A gang plank extended to the shore,
and a beaten trail curved upwards to the county road.
But that was before something serious happened
and the trail was overrun with kudzu,
the plank sinking into the river. This occurred
right after the Berlin Wall collapsed. Neighbors renewed
their interest, and wagered his career failed
with the cold war, a disconnect no doubt
from the CIA. He spoke Czech, you see,
received letters, addressed in a clear feminine hand
from Prague of all places. When the letters stopped,
KGB agents, identified by their non-descript Renaults,
crept slowly up the county road,
searching for the path overgrown with green.
The truth of the matter (from a Bohemian source)
claimed Otto had taken to writing
children's stories about talking cats.
They were being published in the Czech Republic
under the nom de plume of a beautiful
young blonde named Freda Horst.

Touch

The cat follows her
into the kitchen
hours before dawn
while the neighborhood
sleeps. He stares
blankly at his bowl,
not expecting
anything more
than his *Fancy
Feast*. Rain
has been dripping
from the eaves
since midnight,
running down the
screen like lines
in a Braille romance.
No one sees
how her bedroom's
finger of light,
motionless
on the lawn,
holds the page
for any to touch;
her affair
is kept fiction,
driven
only by plot,
a story of blind
protagonists
and a cat.

Cataract Love Poem

I help you tape
a plastic shield
over your eye. We
make sure the ad-
hesive is smooth
against the
sensitive parts
of your face,
forehead, nose,
a slice of cheek,
no more. Sleep
will not come
easily as it is.
The thought of
surgery still
foreign to us,
a subject that
our parents broached
in the kitchen,
along with stories
of broken hips,
stroke and gout.
All the cells in
your body are re-
placed, made new
every seven
years. You are
young. Tomorrow
you will see.

II. Turned Against the Sleet

Farm Notes

Afternoon brings early ice.
Took the stock trailer to Gilpin's
new auctioneer. Old man

Gilpin's down with gout, done
with livestock. Cut out a few head
to get through the winter.

Stopped for gas at Bo's. Shelby
walked in with Maria on his arm.
She set our boy on the counter

while she fished through her bag
for cigarette money. The boy has
mom's eyes. I can see them

clear as the photograph
on Pop's nightstand. She asked me
if I was a big-time country star, yet.

I asked her if she thought the boy
knew me. She handed Bo a five
and said probably not

I was just another
stranger to him. No words
for that. She took her change

and left. The boy watched me
all the way to the car. Shelby
nodded, followed them out,

collar turned against the sleet.
We leave for Terlingua next week.
Maybe meet the guy from

Mesa Records. Snow and ice
comes early. Won't last with the dirt
still holding October sun.

Winter Solstice

The neighbor woman walks out in a red bathrobe,
stooped against the cold, arms folded protectively to her.
She opens the door of the shed and a dozen or more chickens
fly out like leaves blown by a power mower. They swirl

about her legs and then are quickly tossed out of sight
around the edge of the garage. The woman hurries inside
to the coffee she left on the window sill.
Long bars of sun flex across the shadows. The chickens

mill about the lawn, pecking the sunlight from the roots
of the zoysa. Her coffee, fanning a halo of steam
above the sill, rises in the light of the sink;
a small metal chain connects to the bulb.

Winter Dance

Snow spits
against the window,
the furnace clicks in the
crawl space below the
floor and warm air pours
into the living room. It's
not magic; it's mechanics,
simple pragmatism and pre-
dictability: a fire started
in advance in the mouth
of a cave, a plumber crawling
below the floor joists,
running galvanized pipe
through the murk, gas jets,
forced air, heat. Directions
for pilot lighting
painted on the walls.
This said, a woman
dancing through the empty
rooms of the house, her
bare legs tattooed with
the play of light,
excites more
than desire, her grace
in movement sublime,
her beauty not
just a come on.

Subsistence Farming

        The kitchen door
          swings wide
        and his wife appears,
       her arms folded against the chill.
      Snow makes the green
     so very green,
    and she points to the squirrel-ear lettuce
    cropping in bed rows.
    He flails a hand as much to heaven
     as to snow, *Cold*
       will set us back.
      But the curve of her
         warmth comes to him
          and he returns to the house.
         Words fail him in love; they rust
            like garden tools
             and clank against his teeth.
            A well-oiled hoe. Soft
              soil for carrots. Red
              worms and mulch.
              She opens her arms to reply,
               Turnips and radishes,
               potatoes pulled
               from dirt.

Discovering Rose

Not even the oldest neighbor (two
were interviewed)
recalled what this fringe of daffodils
           once outlined.
So for the sake of history, they invented
a plausible, potting shed
with stacks of dank, clay pots,
stacked one inside the other,
leaning (impossibly) into
a shadow of tomato stakes, some
tied with nylon stockings.

A pair of cotton gloves, pinked
with a faded, blossom print
quietly feminine, caressed the lip
of a watering can.
Tools (industriously)
hung on pegboard:
the small spade and the weeding claw
and the iron crowbar for poking
holes for bulbs. All were connected
(poignantly) with cobwebs
in a galvanized bucket.

On the upper shelves, beyond
the curiosity of her cats, stood
brown bottles and dusty cardboard
labeled *Poison.* A sleepy
wasp flitted in the doorway
breeze. She kept a fence (defensively), probably
of painted wire.
Below the fly-specked window squatted
a bushel basket, half-filled
with the neighbor children's stained baseballs
and scuffed plastic Frisbees.

Auction of Small Ghosts

Colonel Banjo the auctioneer
sets up a table of glassware:
green depression, portrait bowls,
hand painted chocolate pitchers,
a Limoges hair receiver;
and then along the hedgerow, he lines
end tables, a marble topped dresser,
slag floor lamps, a mahogany hall tree.
Next to the basement steps squats
a bushel basket of deer antlers,
a stoneware crock of crocus bulbs,
a broken Nu Grape clock, hand tools, milk jugs,
the headlights of a Bel Air,

a cardboard box for the mortician
who collects windup toys,
one for Rose from the junk shop
who buys chipped McCoy,
another for the florist who sells buttons
and postcards on eBay. They bid
for connection to what has passed.
Mr. Garrison the biology teacher
sprays chigger repellent on his ankles
before walking the high grass
to the barn. He shoulders
a flat of faded photographs,
small ghosts smiling through sepia.
Draped over the stock fence,
Colonel Banjo displays
the toe-holed quilt the family
wrapped Terry the schnauzer in
the night he died of heartworm.

Tacitus Silent at Last

The opossum digs through the trash
in the back of the house. The man
hears him tearing paper bags
and nosing cans of ravioli from the night's supper.
A bottle clunks against the concrete sidewalk
and he recalls the wine turned to vinegar,
poured down the sink last week.
Tacitus the terrier yelps, scratching at the kitchen door
and clicking his nails against the linoleum.

He rolls half a Xanax in cheese,
and drops it in the dog's bowl.
He slips open the study window and eases out
onto the porch roof, gingerly settling the Johnny Walker
against the familiar shingles. He has duct taped
his Eveready flashlight to the stock of his son's
BB gun. The opossum settles.
The man fears he has waddled off across the alley.
So he waits, staring at the remains of his marriage
strewn down the sidewalk. Now, with Tacitus silent,
maybe he can hear. Any of those paper bags
could hide the truth.

Thomas Paints a Fence

A praying mantis the size of Tom's fingernail
creeps an inch from the new paint. He takes
the tip of his putty knife and lifts it
free before it's engulfed in latex, imprisoned

like a mosquito in Baltic amber. Lightly,
he blows it into the blades of pampas grass.
When he spreads another brush load,
a second and a third mantis

ride up over the lip of the post.
He doesn't remember seeing a nest
so he begins to search the length of fence,
brush in bucket, hands on knees, head tilted,

eyeing every thorn of weathered wood.
When he shakes out his brush to begin again,
each stroke begins with a quiet breath,
a fingertip in a wound.

Ramsey Recalls His Fear of Snakes

Mr. Ramsey suffered with pins in his foot, his cast
cushioned on a stack of books. He had remained
comfortable in his Methodism, even when faced
with his fall from the church-house steps.
However, he recalled a summer in Alabama
his family had gone to dig coal from the deep mines.

They were proselytized by evangelists in a camp
behind the bowling alley. Below the balmy awning
a serpent-handler brought down all manner of nightfall
on to the heads of sinners.
As a boy he watched his uncle's conversion,
his knees in the dirt, the pebble of tongues in his mouth,
a moccasin writhing below the string
of bare-lit bulbs. A southern wind lapped
at the canvas like a dog at a water bowl.
The young Ramsey held tightly to the seat of his wooden chair.
He feared that he might be called to rise

into the aisle, wrists in the air, hands like tent flaps,
a snake heavy coiling on his shoulders like a muscle.

A Mother's Omen

Mother dreams her daughter is swimming
With deer. Impervious to the danger
Of drowning, the girl
Grips antlers like the reins of a horse
And rides the flood.

During the night, mother
Rises exhausted, hands clenched. In the kitchen
She drinks from the faucet, rain
Drumming the windows. Finally, before dawn
She makes coffee.

With morning she walks in the pelting rain
To the river with her daughter;
The redbuds, submerged to flowered limbs,
Slap the whitecaps, current
Drowning the footpath.

A chicken coop, uprooted, floats midstream,
Ridden by a single white hen. The bird,
Seemingly unruffled, perches
On a fragment of roofing, asleep to omens,
To dreams of flood,

To the small girl thundering in the mud.

Orion in the Sweet Gum

In the morning light between storms,
a man latches on his galoshes
and emerges with his snow shovel

to scoop sweet gum balls
into the back of his Ford Ranger.
The neighbor in the flowered housecoat

leans from her doorway to retrieve the
morning news. She shuts the door
directly. Her gray cat

slips out in the shutting, and preens himself
as a king. Nuthatches and sparrows
chirp in the icy rain that

has begun to fall. By mid-morning,
the man finds himself ladder perched
with the cat on a limb, aloof

in the icing rain, the heroism
of cat catchers barely tenable.
He releases his grip from

the branch, balancing his rubber boot
at the center of the aluminum rung,
then his body swings into the steep sky,

an Orion in the Sweet Gum, cat
strangling in one hand,
women weeping.

Pick-up

A rat in the grass outside the deli
picks through the salting of snow, flips
a leathery pepperoni with his claws
and wedges it into the slit of his mouth.

Two boys with a basketball,
heading home from the playground,
cross the drive-through to the curb.
The rat darts for the shelter of the sewer.

One boy heaves the basketball after him.
It skips on the pavement
and rebounds off a gas meter,
lodging like the shadow of a planet

between the gutter drain
and the snow-wet branches. The rat
rises, ball in his court.
The boys edge shoulder to shoulder

into the drift of sodden leaves.
They stoop with their hands
wedged in their hoodies:
ball within reach, weather

picking up, sleet in the face
beginning to sting.

Tuning Her Guitar at the Safe House

She uncovered the old
Gibson at a Joplin
pawn shop. She practiced
new chords
for months, callusing
her fingers fret by fret,
a new song for each
of his moods,
until finally
the strings
tightened to breaking
bent the neck
to a vibrating twang,
and when the bridge separated,
the only action possible
was a twist on the truss rod
and new strings
of lighter gauge.

Bumper Sticker

Her ex's dog she keeps, but later dumps
on account he is insensitive (chews
furniture, pisses carpets, jumps fences
for bitches). One day he passes her

in the back of a pickup truck.
Their eyes lock through a red light.
On the back of the truck a bumper sticker
reminds her that *Dogs Are People Too*

in DayGlo green. This gives her pause
to revisit the guilt she's carried
since she left him with a cocktail waitress
at Lefty's Steakhouse, who in turn

passed him down, bone for bone,
like a re-gifted wedding blender
to the first cowgirl she met
who wasn't afraid of a little crazy.

Digging Up the Septic Tank

Repairing the septic tank
in summer heat
is serious work for an old man;
his neighbors shout
from air conditioned Fords
that he's crazy to be out in this.
Waving his iced tea,
he takes a cut of baling wire
and sinks it to find soft soil;
several times he clips the spool,
narrowing a circle until he strikes
the top of the tank.
He rings the perimeter
between virgin rock and turned soil
with wire spears; he squares
a folding chair
next to the garden. With a spade
and a sharp shooter,
kept oiled in the barn, he parcels
the repair down to concrete and tar.
His eyes rest on prize
tomatoes, rooted into the
lateral's current, untouched
by drought.

Applause for Widow Audubon

Mud-deep in her husband's boots
she spills sunflower seeds
into the feeder. Starlings
dot the lawn, truculent and greedy.

She slaps the metal scoop
against the trash lid, shakes
a can of WD-40
and sprays the feeder pole
to slow the squirrels.
Tonight's applause
is late for Widow Audubon;
she works alone,
December shadows barring
the lawn like a cage.

Wheel of Fortune, her
favorite, spins through
the kitchen window, flickers
off a 50 gallon storage drum,
galvanized against rust, tightened
against mildew. Once
they had time, the two of them
for television, for sunflower seeds
protected they thought
forever in a metal can.

Neighbors Don't Understand

On her fortieth birthday she
takes a corn knife, honed
like a barber's razor. She has
highlighted a yellow zigzag
across her wrist,
an old scar, a template, the kind
metaphors bleed through in fiction.
The corn knife rests at her feet.
She does all this in the trees
near the creek where she
speaks freely, her audience
dependably detached, a crow
on a limb, a bird
keeping secrets; silence
purchased for corn.

Poem for Sale

He begins before the
bullet, the pills, the
rope to give away
what he holds
in the creases of his clothes.
He empties his pockets
on the nightstand,
hears a few coins
clatter on wood.

Michael Hogard's Wake

The happy hour from Chubb's Bar
kneels shoulder to shoulder: dominoes

with bare fists, stiff shoes, and spiked
pocket hankies. Rosary beads

rattle against the pew like knuckles.
The prayers, memorized at St. Mary's,

have grown unfamiliar. They recite them
as slurs of inarticulate vowels,

growled RRRs, and sputtered Ts. Sister Anna
still watches, frowning as their

butts rest on the pew like a barstool,
a first sign of the devil's sloth, and then

the second back at Chubb's, when Tom Burns
twirls his finger for another round.

III. Bucket and Broom

Buddhists Call It Monkey Mind

Take toothpaste for instance
white foam splattered
on the mirror, on the vanity,
on the chrome faucet.
Each time you spit,
lather drips down your chin,
runs the brush onto your hands;
you can smell mint
the rest of the day on your fingertips.
When you woke
that morning, you were just
another sap with halitosis;
by noon, you're a reformer.
Purpose evokes response.
You begin to petition.
A man, calling himself a friend,
stops you on the street,
and asks to suck your fingers,
to lick your cuticles.
You lend him a hand.
At first, he is gentle, tentative.
Before long, he is stuffing
your knuckles, hands, wrists
into his mouth like sausages.

Cinderella

She's so very tiring
In her thread-bare peasant smock,
Her poor-me pout,
And self-absorbed
Pumpkin paranoia.
She's a bitch, moping
Around the fireplace
With her little bucket
And broom. Troubled,
Brooding on rescue.
All the while
Living on favors from
A fairy godmother
Who trades in Victoria's
Secret Miracle bras, matching
Thongs, thigh-high
Gartered stockings. It's enough
To make a wicked, glamour-
Deprived, step-sister weep.
Glad that at long last
She's found a prince
And dropped-off her
Goddamn glass slipper.

Hansel and Gretel Get the Word on the Street

You have tried leaving
a trail of bread crumbs
that will take you
back home to father,
but the grackles
eat them as soon
as your little sister
quits shooing them away.

The rest of the story
is scarier. There's
a witch at the edge of town
who will lock you
in a rabbit hutch.

She plans
to eat you, once
you're fattened up. After
which, the plot turns
confusing. I've
blocked it out

on account of the
violence, but I know
that you are pressured
to eat fast food: French
fries, hamburgers, chocolate
shakes. You're
required to stick
a bone, rather than
your finger through
the chicken wire.

Of course, only a moron
would confuse
a chicken bone for a finger,

but the word on the street
says you have to fake
your weight-gain. Eventually,
you'll catch the witch
off-guard. Then,
you slip out of the hutch,
push her in a pot
of boiling canola, and
get this, you eat her
candy house.

The witch, they say,
is mostly blind, probably
in the late stages of
macular degeneration. She has
lost her glasses,
and that's another part of
the story that I just
can't digest. The old
lady is shrewd.
She has chewed up little
boys like you for years.
I mean WTF,
she works chat rooms.

She deploys multiple
user-names like Sweet Thing,
Tootsie Roll and Honey Buns.

Lorca Deep Fries a Turkey

Whoever dreamed
peanut oil could change a life?
The first rule: never use
a frozen turkey.
Google it…a family moves
into the street in their stocking feet,
November rain like bullets, children
stricken, parents wide-eyed.
Through the dining room
window, as if orchestrated
by a surrealist, they watch
the table, crystal gleaming,
flatware polished, the antique tablecloth
catching fire at the corners.
The cook should have been reading
directions rather than Lorca.
He was back in Spain, fascinated
with flowers, challenging the heat,
his body a banquet
of fresh bread, mashed potatoes,
oyster stuffing.

Change Comes to Cabbage

after a print by Doris Lee

Imagine seeing the first helicopter
thumping above the family farm,
rotors slicing the air like an Emerson fan.
Blossoms blow from tomatoes.
Dogs bark. Chickens
like straw hats are blown
into the milking barn. A woman
holds court in her kitchen.
She claims an auspicious omen
has broken the silence of the fields.
At long last she speaks her mind.
She packs a suitcase come morning.
Wild geese fasten their bills
to the ropes of her hair and lift her
above the tired cabbage.

Passage to Saturn

The rings of Saturn inspired
His imagination. He turned to them often
In his *Child's Glossary of Planets*. He would trace
Their colors around the page of the book,
Wishing he could fly through space.
He saved for a telescope
With money hoarded from mowing lawns, all summer
Stuffing dollars in a tube sock.

The raven haired girl in the balcony of the Fox
Had been kissed before. She was wise
To boys, spontaneous and alert.
When he turned his head to kiss
Her cheek, her lips were waiting,
Moist and warm as popcorn butter.
It was the most startling moment
Of his life, and she turned him in circles.

He found that summer that the rings of Saturn
Were not solid, but a band of dust
And light refracting debris, particles held by gravity
And pulled by centrifugal spin. The planet
He saw through his telescope, was not
A place to land a rocket.
It didn't matter, even if he cut
A lot of lawns or owned the spaceship.

Boys Dig Through Neighbor's Trash Only to Become Beset by Great Mystery

Why did the neighbor
sisters wrap their

used Kotex
in aluminum foil
and store them
all away
in an oversized
burlap-colored suitcase,
leaving them on the back
porch when they moved?

What led Wally and I,
snooping as boys do
after a neighbor moves,
to swoop through
their belongings like
two gusts of spring wind?

Was it this find that later
drew Wally into anthropology
to dig
through equally mysterious ruins
for tampons of
the Anasazi, and maxi-pads

of Amazons?
What became of the Mayans?
Did they evolve elaborate
astronomical calendars, only
to have them defined
with a period?
Did Atlanteans use string?

And to what do I owe my poetry,
if not to the inspired flow
of the Muses, the great mystery
of the female, opened to me
at such a green age,
wrapped in shining foil,
bearing the blood of life.

After Johnny's Drug Overdose, Wally Keeps His Memory Alive By Begging Cookies at Truck Stops

Wally would go in
pretending to be retarded.
We'd call him Johnny,
order his food, set
his silverware, and dab
his mouth with napkins.
He'd beg like crazy
for cookies, clapping
his little seal
hands and slobbering
his Sunday special
across the table.

Begging for cookies
he'd prop
his head on the
vinyl booth,
food crumbs drooling
into the lap of the
grandmother behind him.
Cookies he'd beg the
neon diner. Cookies
he'd beg the midnight
rednecks
bending coffee spoons
around middle fingers.
Cookies he'd cry
to the flabby armed
cooks and blue haired
cash register ladies.
Cookies he'd mumble
to a crooning Hank Williams
on the chrome juke.
Cookies he'd beg
for Johnny who was dead

and for the Johnnys
who lived
and for the Johnnys who were
caught
not knowing and cookieless.

And sometimes the waitresses
would feel sorry
and other times not
but when they did
they handed over cookies
like they were each
warm nippled breasts,
soft, hand-held and dipped in pink.
But we'd step in
and give them back saying

cookies ain't
good for the boy.
He's got teeth in his head,
not gums.
And we'd leave him

cookieless in
the booth to pretend cry
as we walked off into the gravel parking lot
giggling at our joke.

Wally would rise
quietly like a family
man and pay the bill,
asking for his change
in just ones or fives or some odd amount,
and he might mention how
last week's rain
was just something

perfect for the milo,
and then he'd leave

everyone blank
and speechless
like a dozen open drains

and go floating off
into the night
the way Johnny did.

No Account Gordon

The baby Jesus was a rubber doll,
One whose eyes would flip open when you lifted him
And drop closed when you laid him flat.

The manger was a toy crib
Or a painted cardboard box.
It didn't matter in 5th grade,
Since drama was art, and art was taught
Every Friday after lunch, and
According to Sister, the baby Jesus
Could be found in anything anywhere anytime,
And was certainly no illusion, no way no how.

Gordon, however, bounced a basketball
From the moment he left home
Until he entered
The school playground. Then he stood
Where the four square courts were painted

And dribbled even more.

In November, when Sister cast the Christmas play,
He was chosen to be
One of the three wise men, a real Magi,
Aloof, star-gazing, accountable only
To his inner vision.
He moved in December
To Phoenix, a faraway, desert place.

We didn't see him again until high school,
When he returned to town
Essentially unrecognizable
In his black leather jacket,
Beatle boots and tight jeans. The boys
Traded him high-fives.
The girls, who thought him weird in grade school,

Saw him as dark and mysterious
With his wonderfully banged hair,
His wise lips, his open
Kiss me Jesus eyes.

While Taking Tickets at the Drive-In Theater, Wally Discovers the Cost of Chivalry

One night this cowboy wheels into the Drive-In with his headlights pointing skyward to the moon, rear end clipping speed bumps, muffler dragging. Wally is taking tickets below the marquee, so he steps up to the window to get the money but there's no one in the car, except a skinny-assed driver surrounded by a dozen voices escaping from the headliner, the air vent, the ashtray, the cigarette lighter, all speaking crazy-fast in something like Spanish or Comanche.

Wally thinks about you, Miss Ticket Girl in the mini skirt, perched on your stool by the cash drawer. The driver smiles and Wally takes his cash, pretending like he doesn't see the scam. What if he challenges? And the trunk latch clicks and a dozen tough guys from the road crew climb out with stilettos and switch blades and shining white teeth, and what if they only have enough money between them for one popcorn and a drink. Think about it, what if the two of you would have to chip in, buy all those tough guys tickets, popcorn and root beer, and then, you'd have to sit with them through an entire spaghetti western. You in the backseat. Wally in the trunk.

Teen Age Jesus

Jesus came home one afternoon
while his mother was cooking fish
she'd bought from the Simon Brothers.
Are you making plans for tonight
with that Magdalene girl? She asked.
Jesus shrugged, She's cute, mom,
but I think we're better off
just as friends. Besides,
I'm hanging with Lazarus tonight.
He's been in a dark place since Passover.
We're meeting cousin John
for locusts and honey. He knows a place
down by the river where
they serve them up on platters.

Merit Badge

One of the younger boys started crying.
He couldn't explain his sadness,
the long shadows, the rain clouds
building blue and bruised on the horizon,
the evening sun a slanting saber.
The troop sensed it, loneliness
from hiking beyond what they knew.
The scoutmaster had told the story
of blood that reigned from the river
to the grove of hardwoods. The boys
traced the massacre with footfall
through green briar and wearied ash
tethered with grape vine.
The young Buffalo soldiers,
cheek bones flattened
on Springfields, squinted
down the barrel of the Texas Road.
Quantrill and his blooded riders
pounded into their sights, rising
from the horizon like thunderclouds.

On Christmas Morning at Mother's You Wait in Line to Use the Bathroom

Your wife hunts for her Santa earrings,
by spilling her jewelry across the vanity.
Your youngest complains about her bangs
while retrieving a text message
from a niece in Texas. It includes a photo
of a new baby; the girls cluster like pigeons
between the sink and the stool.
From the window, your son
emerges from the bushes,
twirling a roll of toilet paper.
He is smoking a cigarette and whistling.
You consider driving your car
to the local Convenience Mart.
It's only six blocks. Open on Christmas.
You'll be back before cinnamon rolls.

Old Boy

Wally didn't own a shotgun, but he'd
recently found three tennis rackets
in a dumpster behind the sport's club.

They were wooden, still strung with catgut,
one had a sweat stained leather grip.
All three were perfect for hunting ducks.

When Wally applied for his duck stamp,
the state said, what the hell do you mean
you're going to hunt ducks with a racket?

What kind of ducks, pintails, canvasbacks?
Wally replied that one duck was
as good as the next, but he preferred fowl

that flew within three feet of his blind, those
slower than the rest who had
grown apathetic to migration, and were

content to laze around the refuge, semi-
retired and prone to windy monologues
on the plump hens they'd known.

The Proper Fish

If she would uncover one breast,
and then lower her nipple
into the fishbowl,

I could be koi.

Goldfish below Ice

Frozen, the surface of the pond
is like the screen of an Etch A Sketch:
blank, gray, and expectant.
Goldfish, slow-gilled, float
inches above the mud, aware
of only their connection to depth.
When the ice catches the right slant of sun,
a little color surfaces; as if shimmering
from deepest sleep, gold promises.

Goldfish with the Faces of Old Men

The carp in the Chinese restaurant
wear the faces of old men. They swim
entire lifetimes behind glass, circling
above colored rocks, wiggling below

a porcelain bridge that leads
to a plastic clam shell. There is also
a diver with a helmet, his hand is raised
as if signaling a discovery.

He has dropped from a boat on the surface
where three red faced seaman
carefully check for kinks in the air hose,
minding the rattling air compressor

with careful eye. One man is the leader,
he wears a stained skipper's cap
and leans out over the sun-bright sea.
He is aware of the strain of complacency,

he cautions the others to feed
the hose out slowly. Having seen
the bottom before, the odd faces,
the colored stones, the bridge

that connects the Chinese restaurant
to the slow moving fish, to the boat
on an invisible sea.

Crisp

Boys play football
on Railroad Avenue,
running down-and-outs
from the hydrant
to the light pole.
On the bungalow
porch, old Remy
refinishes a washstand.
On game days, he coaches
from the steps,
scrubbing the oak grain
with quadruple ought
steel wool. He erases
water stains and specks
of paint. The boys
use his sidewalk as
the goal line. He
salutes catches
with a turpentine rag.
Each touchdown
he snaps the air.

IV. New Start in a Meat Wrapper

Performing the High Wire

Before Easter a teacher sent you to the office
where the lady from the *Children's Fund*
presented you with a brown package of clothes.

Walking back to the classroom, you hid
the embarrassment of carrying your
New Start in a meat wrapper. You learned early
that a joke at your own expense

put you in command of effacement. As class clown
you assumed a persona, the package like a chair
on the tip of your nose, tight roping an imaginary high wire
to your desk. You swayed above the eyes
of your classmates, teetering

like nothing mattered but the circus.

Beans from Apple Butter

for Tomaso Ortolani

The boss gives me job to carry the hod.
Me! Un maestro! I lay finest stone in Napoli.
When I come from boat with Giuseppe, they say,
cement mortar, always keep coming.

Then one day I eat lunch, always same
the sardines the bread the black olives,
and I see bosses in circle, brick men
pointing, shaking fingers, pointing more.

I put sardine down on newspaper, and go
to shouting, and I know, problem like snap.
Laying brick in curve, big trouble. Boss ask,
Who knows beans from apple butter?
This is bean. I look him in eye. Now,
I make apple butter, so smooth the cement,
gaps in brick growing, how you say, personality
like teeth in smile, and I point to mouth
no string no level.

The boss puts hands in pockets. He watches,
chewing the cigar, always chewing.
Brick curve like something beautiful
like woman, you see. I step back. How
these apples I ask? Boss smile a little bit.

Hire the butter man. He tap
my brick with clipboard.
After this, I always bring the salami the prosciutto.
No more sardines,
not even today, one hundred years later.

Union

When the jail door shut,
The Benelli brothers bullied their ham-like fists
For one more round with the guards. They cussed
The bosses, the scabs and the cops.

The very afternoon the brothers battled the bars
Their old man dropped from a heart attack,
Digging clams in the Cold Harbor muck.
He rose to one knee, ocean streaming down his back,
Salted hair glistening like nightfall.
Their mother in her long, twilight coat hoisted,

Fighting to keep them above the tide.
The two of them, wide-eyed, cursing God,
Buried their fists in the sea.

Papa's First Trumpet

There was no way during the depression that they could afford it
But somehow his old man came home with a trumpet

And said, son, now you can learn to play it like you want.
He must have sold something like tires from the Dodge
That was jacked up in back

Or a box of black market jackets from old Salvatore.
So get your trumpet Alfred and play us a song.

Go into your room, get the horn
And then play for Uncle Johnny and Aunt Gussie.
Let them hear what we have bottled inside us,

How we've been made to scrape out a life from buttered spaghetti
When we should be artists, drawing and painting and dancing

Like we did before the squeeze box became the banker.
Play your trumpet. That way they can all see

What we're really made of. And so he'd play
The one song they liked
And then others he just made up in his head

The dented brass bell bending the new notes
To stretch between the chairs and curl up to the window screen

Like smoke on the sill in the evening air.

Studied Traffic

Maria gave me a new suit
for Walter's funeral. If dad
had known, he would have
booted her charity
onto Railroad Avenue
where Walter was found. Dad said,
it was wrong for Maria
the-know-it-all to butt in
to a family's trouble. Mom
had ideas: resurrect
Walter's argyle, his oxfords,
his waist-nipped Fred
Astaire jacket, his teen age
love of swing. She feigned thrift
at second hand sales and Uncle
Sal's black market. Maria
ushered me to Mass, assured me that
Walter was safe with the angels.
She held a finger to her lips
and slipped quarters
into my pocket. At bedtime
I pushed Walter's picture
into my new shoe. I counted
quarters. From the porch
Dad studied traffic.
Each sedan on the avenue
passed through a fist of light.

.

The Only Photograph of the Boy as a Child

The boy, hands stuffed in his coat pockets,
Stares at the camera shyly, as if he didn't know
If a smile was allowed. It was a funeral photograph,
Taken when his brother was found,
Killed on Pulaski by the hit and run. The family
Was turned out of bed that night by pounding on the door.

After Pop heard the news, he thanked the police
And ordered the white-haired Priest
To back off of his front porch and
To take his child killing God with him.
In the winter that followed, the boy and his sister
Ate at the table in the kitchen.
Father took his supper
With his silence, alone in the dining room,
Where the daylight hung a minute longer behind the shutter.
Mom brought beer in a corked gallon bottle.
It was a little flat and a little warm. They might
Sit together to drink it and they might not.

Renting a Chicken

Sometimes the old man returns from the market
With a basket of eggs
And he puts them in a crate in the basement,
An arm's length from the furnace.
Then he rents a chicken from Aunt Gussie for sitting.
As a little boy, my job is to feed handfuls of spaghetti
To whichever chicks hatch.

I take one of Uncle Sal's black market coats
And go down with nothing else on underneath.
It's a cold bitch in the morning
Until I crack the ice from the cellar door.

The heat from the basement, oily and sweet,
Smacks my face like stepping into a greenhouse,
And I shake with fear that the smell hangs on me
All the way to school.
And then where am I? Alone
Stinking like a chicken?

Momma sells most of them.
One or two we keep for Easter dinner.
She pushes their necks down to the ground
And draws a line in the gravel
Right in front of their eyes,
Extending from their beaks to whatever horizon
A chicken sees. They hold still
Even for the axe.

Animals We Kept

Nonna kept parakeets. She slipped
thimbles of beer into their water, and they
spoke Italian to her. Cages
hung across the porch on metal hooks
until birds swayed in the wind like lamps.
One Friday, my brother
bulldozed a tree next to Mango's Market.
A nest of squirrels flipped from the branches.
Mother raised the babies in a box
that smelled of peaches. Two died
the first night. Two nursed,
sucking on a scrap of cloth soaked in sugar-milk.

One grew to live in the house,
climbing into Mother's blankets,
burrowing as if to heartwood.
The dog belonged to me.
The old man said the mutt was a turd eater.
I found him tied to a mailbox next to the YMCA.
He ran off once after a garbage truck,
and I chased him
until the streets turned dim
and the faces on the porches grew curious
about the lost boy with the lost dog.
I curled up next to the Boxing Club,
my hand twisted in the dog's collar.

Some nights, the old man
would hike with Uncle Sal to the city dump
to hunt rats with the twelve gauge,
bagging a bottle of wine, maybe some bread.
I'd wake when they stumbled through the door,
smelled their clothes thick with wine and trash smoke,
dragging their heavy boots
across the porch, batting
the cages like speed bags, cursing
the squirrels, my dog, the rats
as big as a dog, the rats
as big as a boy.

Sometimes the End is a Beginning

We take our sleds
and hide in drifts
behind parked cars.
Then, we run through the snow
after the first car
to turn
onto Railroad Avenue.

Johnny Vacca grabs
the bumper, then Stevie
Grant takes hold of
Johnny's boots, followed
by me and little Arnie,
then whoever's fast
enough to link up. Fat
William is always last.
Now, he's a tug. Nearly
jerks the arms out
of our sockets.
If we are really slick,
the driver drives on
about his business, unaware
of the train of kids
snaking through the traffic.

But always, someone
gets pissed and swerves,
trying to shake us off.
This is the best ride,
holding until our fingers
freeze like claws, slamming
into curbs, parked cars,
cops blowing whistles.
Who knows? A bunch
of dumb kids without
a nickel between them.
Danger. Hell, it is 1939.
Snow lasts forever.

Shoveling Snow at the High School

The principal sat in his window
and watched through the blinds.
The snow had fallen heavily.
We had skipped school,

gone down to the city barn
and waited for shoveling jobs.
The foreman, old bastard we called him,
sent us right back to the high school

to clean the sidewalks.
The blinds parted and old man Thompson
cracked the window
and called us into the office. We stood

dripping slush and mud
as he chewed us out, up one wall
and then down the next, for not
learning our English and our math.

Then he'd have the secretary
bring in hot chocolate and we'd sit
blowing the steam through our hands
until we could grip a pencil again.

First Night with Cyclones

Put'em up, Alfred,
  this bad boy is
   coming for you, shouts Mac
    the Pencil Head.
     Sloppy Frank shoves
      the barrel with his boot.
      A cannon-baller
       rolls from the dock,
       lumbering the ramp,
      shooting cyclones
     up from the planks.
   Alfred lowers his shoulder
  like his buddy, Doyle the Douche,
 but he's plowed, flattened
 like pizza dough.
  Ragged
    and spine twisted,
     he chokes back the tears,
      cusses as big
       as the office foreman.
       Doyle handles the roll,
        eases the barrel upright.
        Dust yourself off, son.
        Those clowns,
          and he nods with his chin
          at Mac and Frank,
           don't mean you real harm.
            They're just a couple
            of blowhards, good
            for the nightshift and
            dicking around,
             but just the same,
             get ready, they're
             likely to
             roll you
              another.

95

Dear Badass,

On the field trip to Cold
Harbor, classmates loved
how you slipped away
from old lady Murphy's
field trip. You rowed
the stolen boat out to
the sandbar, skulled
to the whale's eye,
then, with oars locked, you
posed as if fishing,
catching the great joke
of the semester. The boat
rocked in the beached
humpback's
wake, a dying
flotsam in the ebbing
of the bay. Each time
the tail crashed, the boat
spun. You grabbed the
gunnels, belly laughing
like nothing mattered.

Sincerely, Un-
Convinced

The Gift

The old man had this car that was jacked up in the back yard.
I have no idea where he got it, maybe payment
For some black market job with Uncle Frank.
It was a 1935 Dodge without wheels. One day
Out of nowhere he gave it to me.
He said do whatever.
I couldn't believe my luck,
So I bought some jet-black paint and brushed it
Carefully under the trees. You really had to look
To see the marks. Then I went down to the junkyard
And worked out a deal with Tommy. I lugged home four wheels
And four bald white walls.
One morning the old man
Took a look at what I'd done, and decided that he
Needed the car after all.
So that was that. But sometimes in the afternoon
When he was asleep after the nightshift,
Mom would help me push it
Out of the driveway into the street. Before supper,
She would follow me back in with a rake, smoothing the gravel
Over the tire tracks.

Deep on Punt Return

He recognizes the tenor in his father's voice
Booted above the noise of the crowd,
The sugar in his booze unmistakable.
The town has seen the old man fumble,
Carrying his kid in the curve of his arm,
Seldom tucked, swinging
Wildly like a loaf of bread. On weekends
He can be flagged at the top of the bleachers
With his mouth open, his arm cocked,
His great coat buttoned to his throat.
Waving off the fair catch, his son
Gathers himself between the hashmarks,
Waiting as the ball drops in the lights
Where once again he takes the hit.

During Hard Times, the Boat Maker Resorts to Football Helmet Repair

The boat maker examined each football helmet
With a shake of his head, "What I won't do for a buck."
Then whispering "Sweet Jesus,"

He hung them on hooks screwed to the ceiling,
Cracked temples and shattered crowns. Coach
Jabbed with his finger, "The guy that wore that one

Is worse off than the helmet," The boat-maker
Nodded his head vigorously, laughing
A fingernail of ash from his cigarette.

Over the week, he layered the helmets
With patches of fiberglass, a bright red resin.
On Friday, Coach fisted them all

By the facemasks. "Now, they're ready
For the next poor slob." There was
Laughter, more ashes fell. "You should have

Stuck to leather," the boat maker scoffed.
Coach grinned, "Look who's giving advice,
A wop who makes sailboats in Kansas."

The boat-maker pulled deeply on his cigarette,
Picked a twig of tobacco from his tongue,
"Well, there's not many of us."

Tupperware

The GI Bill paid for the first television
and the only window air conditioner
on the block. The mercury rose.
Dad traded
his spare tire for a pedal car
and claimed I drove like Barney Oldfield.

When I left it on the sidewalk, the sun heated
the metal seat, blistering Skip Lazarri's ass.
Our canvas wading pool swallowed
Billy Tanner. When his head went under,
no one noticed, until his mother
stepped into the pool
and yanked
his butch-waxed hair into the sun. He cried
draped in a towel.
One evening after a heavy rain,
the purple sky rumbled
behind the elms. We drug a cardboard
box to the College Lake and filled it
with toads and frogs. Some were small,
the size of grapes. One was like a melon, fat,
petulant and ugly. Old Ferraro
dubbed him El Dulce.
"The bastard," he said. "Put him
in Tupperware. Leave him
on the sidewalk for the sun."

Kite String

The boy had this reoccurring dream
of playing in the front yard
at the old Navy barracks when
for no apparent reason he began
to drift into the sky. He would rise
to maybe twenty or thirty feet
above the head of his mother.
She would stand on the lawn
and demand that he return to earth.
He floated like a kite. He could see
himself in his bed dreaming,
the roof of his house, his shadow
wrinkled on the shingles.

Other times he dreamed that he
was in the Plymouth with his father.
They were on the highway to Joplin,
always on the curve near the drag strip.
His father would be speaking to him,
attention divided between the road
and the word. Then his father
disappeared, and the boy floated alone
in the passenger's seat, just high enough
to see over the dash, the highway
falling away below him,
the steering wheel untended,
quivering, motors
from souped-up hotrods roaring.

When he woke in the dark,
the bathroom light a rectangle on the floor,
he reminded himself that parents
didn't disappear, and boys didn't
float off across the neighborhood
like kites. Strings were wound
tight on spools. The last inches
knotted, tied to last forever.

Legacy

During the night, the wind picks up.
First in the high branches of the walnut
and then in the hanging geraniums.
The neighbor's porch light appears
to move against the screen, swaying,
flickering behind the limbs. The man

in the green house has been up and down
all night. The lights flashing
from room to room; he searches the kitchen
for ibuprofen, then the bathroom. He gives up
and returns to bed. Later, he steps out onto
the porch and digs through his tool bags.

A small job like painting the garage
has turned his knees into battlegrounds.
He listens for thunder in the distance,
rain that will keep him indoors tomorrow,
a respite that doesn't require him to quit
or to give in to pain. He never once

remembers his father quitting,
even at the end, the family gathered,
the cancer stretching into winter.

V. Waving Mustard in Surrender

Waving Mustard in Surrender

I.

Outside the *Big Easy*, the saxophonist
loads his horn into the backseat
of his Dodge. He stops to wipe sweat
from his eyes. Some cat with a white

hat and a blonde on his arm says man
that last number was prayer. Waitresses
danced between tables; cocktails
teetered on black trays. Danny slid

from the kitchen with his washboard
rasping. A flicker rippled the room, neon
crossing bowls of gumbo.

II.

You signed your last email Joey
the Chocolate King, a reference
to Merton's humor. You wrote
about gunshots in the parking lot

at the *Town Topic*, the cook hitting
the floor with a spatula in the air,
the girl at the counter saying it's this way
at hamburger joints the world

over. And you're thinking what kind
of prayer can you add to the ether tonight,
waving mustard in surrender.

III.

At the back of the *Neon Gallery*
barbecue ribs are spread on white
butcher paper. The River Cow Orchestra
sets up in the front window so

anyone from the street can see
the bass player's akimbo arms. Poets
are wedged between performances
like cheese: cheddar Swiss limburger.

Six women in black leotards dance
the floor in their bare feet. Blind Tony
taps time at the door.

A New Arrangement

I.

You were drunk as usual, wine soaked,
swollen with song. The moon like a sponge
floated on the Missouri. Seated on a five
gallon bucket, you recited

your take on Charlie Parker, alone
at Lincoln High School, not yet ready
for the new sound cranking in his head.
For years, you wrote songs

on bar napkins, cleaned them like catfish
and sunk the bones in empties. A sound
like *bebop a-rebop*

II.

toys with your line in the current.
That's why you keep the gig
at your side. Once snagged
you flip the catch into the Coleman's

hissing yellow, moths and June beetles
battering the globe, fish
breaded with cornmeal, peppered
in the pan. Grease pops

in old phrases. Yet, something else
swims the channel,
a new arrangement laid

III.

over an old melody. Heat lightning
at three a.m. You rise from bed
to sit on the front porch. It has not
rained in weeks. So what

if you're in your underwear. An old man
is entitled to fresh, boney knees.
You flash your AARP card at the neighbors.
If any are interested, they can swim

into the sprinkler system, man
and woman, sputtering Bird Changes
in the twelve bar blues.

Heat Wave

I.

I say it's the heat man that keeps
you at Kaw Point. Down at the confluence
of the Missouri, smoking brick
in the shade, a chain of antlers

hanging in a willow like voodoo bones.
You got a line of fishing poles, butt
ends in the mud resting on forked
sticks, set with blood bait for channel cat.

Nothing bites until nightfall, the skyline
louder than stars, helicopters
beating above the streets.

II.

Hotel Muehlebach: taking pictures
where Teddy Roosevelt used to sleep,
this cat pulls a U-turn
and begins to parallel park his Lincoln

into the wheelchair ramp. He wedges
his maroon bumper against my bumper
and the passenger door
opens. A plump, mini-skirted thigh

emerges. Her man, not watching
what we're watching, sits at the wheel
drinking from a sack,

III.

and she with her head high, hips
round and curved in magenta, high heels it
into the air conditioning with what
appears like a job application.

We squeeze out from the curb
and drive on to the ballpark, downing
a twelve back from the floorboards.
It's 104 degrees. *Miller Lite*

costs ten dollars a can at the *K,* and it's
going to be one of those nights, one moment
thirsting after another.

VI. Wax Lips

Seventh Grade Communication Arts

For 25 cents the boy throws
himself across the hallway
and slams his head against the lockers.
He uses the money to buy candy
at the PX across from school.
He shows up in my fifth hour with a bag
of red licorice, wax lips and a welt
on his forehead. He has
a twitch in his eye.
I tap his action verb worksheet.
He slides the sack in his backpack. Later,
I notice the red licorice in his lap.
He's nibbling like a rabbit.
I remind him to put up the candy.
The next time I look
he's wearing the wax lips.
I reach out my and he drops the lips
in my palm. I toss them in the trash.
Hey, he complains. How can I smile
if you trash my lips?

Straining Tea

for M#

I had to admit that she
was the most innovative
teacher I'd ever met, but for
the most part I thought
she talked too much, sounding
a bit like Forrest Gump with her
my momma used to say routine.
Each morning, I'd
sip her green tea between
stacks of student essays,
office announcements, emails
from the Board, the NEA, the District
Coordinator, or the Department Chair.
One day she steeped
the tea without the strainer, the ball

lost somewhere in the juggle of fire drills,
pep assemblies and lunch room supervisions.
Parsley-like flakes floated in a disturbing swirl
to the top of the cup.
She folded our yellow missive on AYP
(Annual Yearly Progress) into
an origami crane.
She slipped it forefront
into her menagerie of paper memos:
dragons monkeys lions.
Momma used to say
she slurped
through a tight smile, green leaves
spotting her teeth.

English Class Angler

"…our sudden thought
of the water shining
under the morning fog"

from a poem of Wendell Berry
checked out as a writing prompt
from the school library

by a boy who'd rather be casting
sleek monofilament from his johnboat
than reading.

He writes of strip pit water at dawn,
the wash of silver
that cascades from fish leaping

for mosquitoes
as the dark brightens.
Pole whipping thin light, he stirs

the classroom with quips, casts,
waits for poetry to strike,
to break surface like bass.

The Professor Busts a Local Meth Lab

The professor was known to lose track of himself for hours on end. New Year's Eve was no exception. He had merely driven one block too far to a departmental cocktail and had consequently knocked on the door of a meth lab. The junkie with the forty-five told police in his subsequent six hour stand-off that he had no intention of shooting a professor that night; it was an accident forced by improper residential zoning. Professors, he insisted, shouldn't be barging in on the privacy of a lab; recipes are arguably intellectual property. The girlfriend, still doe-eyed, but lined and creased with hard riding peeked from behind the gun. Doyle, she said, nudging her boyfriend with her forehead. That's the professor who flunked me out of English 101. We got nowhere to run.

Biology Lab

The kids say she's
a bitch. The faculty
speaks of her as a tough nut.
The administration
highlights her student's
test scores. When parents
phone, she explains her goals
for teenagers with
a hopeful, optimistic
diplomacy. At night
she sifts through stacks

of lab reports, red ink
on her fingertips.
Early in her career
she thought
a perfect score might
change the world.
Tonight, she drinks
too much wine
and draws multi-colored
happy faces
on even
the weakest papers.
Rain loosens the last

leaves. Geese fly south
in football season. She
remembers them chattering
below the clouds like
cheerleaders.

Walking the Cemetery with a Three Year Old

The frontage road to the Dairy Queen spills with traffic,
so my grandson and I walk the shortcut through the cemetery.
We discover an open grave, unfinished, yawning
before a beleaguered backhoe. We toss clods

from the mound to the layer of clay at the bottom.
He asks about fire trucks and motorcycles.
He listens to the street: sirens and horns and tires squealing.
I hear the silence in each clod's fall and the thud at the end of the arc.
I ask him to tune his ear to the quiet, to the gravity in falling.

Instead, he questions the defunct backhoe, the oil blackened casing,
the cables unplugged and dangling like bereft fingers.
He sits in the scoop and digs,
the shovel of his heels lifting the dirt.

Listening for Bees in the Floor of the Old School House

for Dorothy Collins

Your mother's voice grew
feint like the stirring
below the floor. You put

your head to her chest
and heard the emptiness
which followed her last

heartbeat, and there
you hung, your body
stretched as if across

a cool oak floor, your ear
pressed to the wood,
unable to distinguish

the silence between you
and the bees and the
silence which grew then

between you and her,
her breath a wind
escaping through a door.

Among Bees

for Bev Corcoran

Imagine bees leaving the hive
one bright morning
and then returning at dusk only to find
the supers moved, hauled
by the keeper's truck
to some undisclosed field. The bees
fly pollen laden
until exhaustion sets them down
alone in their simple beeline, disoriented,
estranged from the hive, the one truth
still burning in their wings.

The local newspaper reports: teachers,
social workers, artists, crawling through fields,
speaking in low whispers to the lost.
The government pledges
in the taxpayer's best interest
to have the State disconnected

from the cost of rescue: shutting down
funding for bee soup lines, worker
re-education centers, 501c3s
for drones
in need of a queen.

The Teacher Canoes through 7th Hour

The teacher dreams of skipping school,
canoeing into a fold of Ozark green
and drifting where the daylight pools
in slips of river and seamless trees.
He thinks to slow time, to paddle stroke
beyond broken thoughts, weaving
poetry through the splatter of oaks.
In the forest he will be free
instead of capsized beside the coffee pot,
folding paper boats out of high school rhyme,
flotsamed like leaf meal on the desktop.
His students chatter, adrift in the wild
currents of spring: love letters in glitter glue,
Kool-Aid colored hair, a heavy metal tattoo.

At-Risk in Bonehead English

Sudden snow blew from the north
like a thin, crisp mistake, white and crystalline,
more powder than flake. Lacking in depth
of grace or beauty, it lay as an indignant
sheet of winter, a threat to the crocus
unfolding below the maple. Perhaps ice
turns me cold in the classroom, focused
on the boy who walks in without a pass
to visit the mouthy girl by the window;
the one whose name is scrawled on desks.
He chews gum, jaw muscles bursting under
pale, thin skin. His eyes dart across
the room, challenging winter:
the bud that flowers in snow.

Tough Cookies

smoke at the bowling alley
on Christmas night.
They bounce on their toes
below the *Open* sign
for warmth.
Swirls of snow brush
down Broadway, multi-colored
lights blinking in evergreens.
Two security employees
from the casino creep
into the bowling alley parking lot.
They drive a beat-up Bronco, windshield
encrusted with sleet—scraped
to two dark slits.
The chains on their tires
jingle across the ice.
The tough girls share
a tube of cherry lipstick.
They check their breath
by singing O Holy Night
into their hands.

Wally Steals Oscar

the lab skeleton
and pranks him, legs crossed,
smoking a Camel Light
in the front row
of Western Civilization.
He throws a white scarf around
Oscar's cervical vertebrae, drapes
one end down the ribcage, the other
over the clavicle, pilot like.
A note taped to the sternum
reads, I am the 100%.
Wally makes a statement
about the economy;
he's always been broke. He
is a believer in sharing,
ashes to ashes, dust to dust
and all that. Turmoil
runs like rain, curb to
curb down Cleveland Street.
Campus Security gathers
outside of Comparative
Anatomy: red lights for
the theft of bones, broken glass.
Wally opens his umbrella
and holds it high
for anyone who wishes.

We shut Eddie
in a refrigerator
because of the Soviet Union.
You see, Eddie had these dull
metal braces, meant to straighten
his weird foot. Our mothers said,
he could be fixed
& no one would see
how he struggled to be normal, so
wouldn't it be neighborly
to include him in the space race?
The ambulance arrived that evening
about the time our Mercury
capsule splashed down in Blakely's lot.
Eddie was strapped on a metal cart;
an oxygen mask gripped his face. He
reminded us a bit of Gus Grissom, only
flat and two dimensional, his
fleecy hair plastered
against his forehead,
the color of the gurney,
the color of his brace,
as silver as the moon.
We saw Eddie
once more that summer
and that was in the backseat
of his parent's Buick on the
4th of July. We were
lighting Black Cats
and tossing them
into lazy missiles
that exploded in mid-flight.
When Eddie passed, it
was cool how he waved,
not with his hand, but with a thumbs up
better than that Russian Yuri guy.
He'd never ratted
& we gave him
credit for that; he was
nearly normal for a gimp.
Eventually, Mr. Blakely
took the door off the Hot Point
& he pushed it
face down in the weeds,
where it orbited the neighborhood
invisibly for years

Bracket for Normal

Birding in Squalor

The amateur
ornithologist
rests on his
shopping cart
under the
garage eave,
hat cocked,
waiting for
the wren
to poke her
head from
the siding's bung
hole. The
Jenny rose
earlier
than the man,
& now, invisible
in the high
wires, scolds him
for missing her
fast wings—her
razor strength,
the white grub
pierced
cleanly
in her beak.

It's a Jungle Out There

The cat slips around
the side of the house
with this little rabbit
in his mouth. The head
of the rabbit inside,
the body hanging
like a sack down his chin.
I grab the cat (his
name is Jasper)
and the rabbit (who is
nameless) falls
to the ground, and then
kicks off towards the
wooden fence. He bangs
into a picket, tries again
and slashes through the
gap into the front yard.
Jasper squirms out of
my arms and jumps
the fence. I trip
on a paving stone and fall
between the rose bushes.
Jasper catches the rabbit
a second time, dangling him
by his spine. I spray him
with the garden hose and he
trots off with the rabbit jiggling
between his teeth. I dive
and grab a fist full of cat fur
(white as a pillow). The rabbit
(still nameless) twists free
and darts under the deck.
I return to watering
the geraniums.
A moment later Jasper
is banging around
in the neighbor's hostas;
the rabbit
back for more.

Brainwashing as Self-Help before Spring Break

Take out your brain and set it on the concrete
At the local carwash, and for seventy-five cents
Hose it down with the soapy water. Fill the folds
Until they've lathered and overrun
The pavement. Then click to rinse,
Finger open wrinkles and shoot them free of yesterday
And the yesterdays before yesterday. Send them
Floating gray and bubbling towards the metal grate.
Try not to listen to the voices, the memories
Popping out of bubbles like plaintive children.
Set your washed brain on the hood of your car
And let it dry in the spring sun. Flip it over a few times
Before dropping it back into your skull.
Do this before you drive, before you begin again.

Three Hundred

Three hundred were taken
away in the night

from the monastery in Ngaba.
Twenty year old Tibetan monk
Phuntsog walked into
the center of the street
and lit his gasoline soaked robes.
Chinese police
beat him with clubs
while he burned. One claimed
they were beating
the flames into submission.
Phuntsog, taken to the
local hospital, was later
kidnapped by a gang of monks
said another official.
His death was duly recorded.

Three hundred were taken
away in the night, whereabouts
unknown.

Noble Silence

A fan squeaks throughout
the noon meditation session,
one of the eight that keeps

the Missouri heat moving
until the chime of the bell.
When we stretch our legs, standing
in our socks on the hard wood, eyes
search the rotating blades
for the culprit, but
the squeak has stopped, each

of us points in a different
direction while we circle
in and out through rows
of cushions, the welcome

silence well-oiled.

VII. Beyond the Bean Rows

Second Rain

The 17 foot Grumman
rests on sawhorses
behind the garage at Golden Age.
Mrs. Vacca's mutt
anchors the frayed blue tarp
in rain storms. The water
that drips off the roof
splatters along the keel
and runs in small rivers
to the paws of the dog. He ignores
the mourning doves
bathing in puddles, tossing
the storm from their wings
in a thin spray. The canoe's
aluminum sidewalls
drum all morning in the new rain,
a hollow bass,
drenched with June.

Canoeing in Ice Storm

A hooded crow shrugs, clenches
and unclenches his talons,
sidestepping to the end of the branch,
the black of his eye slick like glass.
A man and a woman
paddle in a dome of gray,
connected by the conversation of the canoe: the plop
of paddle, the trickle
of keel, the spit
of ice upon the gunnels. The man watches
the vapor of her breath, a cloud of warmth,
a blue jay from a nest.

Hiking Richland Creek

Pushing through sumac
in winter
reminds me how little
I know about belonging,
my boots clumsy, snapping
branches, leaving snow
turned and scarred.

As the sun dips, night is
a hawk taking wing, tail
feathers bathed in twilight.
Drawing shadows in like a cape,
the cold
wings up the valley.
With each new step I am
startled by my loneliness.

Great Blue Heron

Hushed, he
cuts the surface without
a ripple, stalks his reflection
along the fringe of the pond,
composed in assassin's

restraint. Step by step,
his sharp bill poised

among the cattails, he folds
his ungainly legs below
his body, steadies
the long scimitar of his neck
and moves on,
         crossing the water

with the stealth of a cloud.

Deep Wood Koan

A cater-
  pillar
    crosses
  & re-
    crosses
  the black-
jack
  oak.

    All morn-
  ing he
winds
  down-
    ward
  with the
sun.
  Until fin-

    ally,
  stones
&
  lichen
    crawl
  with day-
light.
  The

    bright
  leg
of morn-
  ing
    bristles
     over
  leaf-
fall;

          darkness
disappear-
     ing into
          the mush-
     room's
          slen-
     der
throat.

Unlikely

A mayfly lands on my
computer screen, translucent
wings lined with delicate veins.
Through them, I read the words
of a new poem entitled "Unlikely."
It consists of an observation
on brevity, on a body too light
for muscle, too ephemeral
for wisdom, unlikely
in its minutes of flight
to discover
much about November.

Secrets

Whenever the fire pit cools,
he walks back to the burn pile.
hunting for the right limb, the one
wedged like a memory from the past.
He searches by touch, passing
through the kindling, the cane and vine,
the dank snarl of tree fall.
He burrows through leaf and limb,
layers of history, old storms
tossed into forgiving decay. Each
branch combusts unlike another;
the flames smolder; the smoke follows
when he moves his chair.

Reading William Stafford in a Snowstorm

His lines are plowed evenly,
Yet I can seldom predict
Where they will break into drifts.
Here by the bookshelf
Then there by the window
    And last, by the blown-open door

Where suddenly I am falling
With the wild driving snow to
Some dark road in Kansas
Which in narrowing its shoulders
To a footpath
    Catches me

Shallow like a snow angel, then
Sinking deeper in
The great, cold billows, I find depths
Made for burrowing
Snow caves
    Beneath the howling night.

Fletching

A hiker sets his Minolta on the stone
fence. In February's mist, cloud
within cloud, silence
is like a feather in the grass,
as much a part of the earth as of the sky.
He picks up his camera and unsnaps
the lens cap. Somewhere this morning
there is a photograph, a doe retreating,
an image connecting the distant hawk
to the fletching of his heart.

A History of Leaves

The leaves are so wet they
roll up in layers like scrolls
under the pitchfork.
Each veined with a thin,
cuneiform message from
the past season.
A woman calls her children
to brandish an army
of rakes and blue tarpaulins—
she cheers
as they load the sodden leaves
into the pickup bed.
Their demeanor is not that
of antiquarians or bibliophiles
hushed over books in a quiet hall.
They dance in the spotted sunlight
between the empty branches,
between the empty tines
that claw the air.
They sing new songs on the
road to the dump.

Return

Deer slide up the creek from the river
as shadows in the morning,
nosing honeysuckle, rooting
sassafras and McDonald's sacks
from the roadway, emerging
from the woodbine
with the moon in their eyes.

The corporate office must have seen this
when building in the woods:
the silence, the calm morning
exhaled like a breath
out of the night, the deer
catching them in the sunrise with their Starbucks,
returning with their briefcases,
car keys tight in their fists.

Henry's Romance

You wish that the stars
between branches
would turn to berries
so you could pack them home
to the kitchen, bake
cobbler for the people you love
and give them a taste
of your recipe, but each time
you hike out beyond the bean rows,
you sit on a jawbone of limestone.
Your feet are stones
in the cedars. You are committed
like the railway
at the edge of the pond.
There is no way
home from here.

Hawk on the Practice Field

The edge of town is not squared,
its carpentry wearied, twisted
as milkweed in January, each season
tugged by gravity, dissolved by rain,
blown by wind. Change is built on conflict,
the smallest bulb, blackened by freeze,
buoys the tulip above death. It screws
through the packed dirt. The hawk
on the goal post leans
tentatively towards the field mouse
in the uncut grass; the dagger
of wing, the clench of talons.

City Council Hires a Cannon

Tonight, I went running, following
the sound of the starling cannon, fired
from below the trees at Lakeside Park.
Above Jefferson Street starlings
circled in growing flocks. They swept
the tops of the elms. The gun pounded,
growing louder, less familiar.
Starlings rose and fell with each report,
pushed to distant trees
by a force they could not fathom.
I ran through puddles from the evening's rain,
the reflection of the sky
splashing beneath my shoes.

Sunday Ducks

Three ducks walk the parking lot
at Brahm's Ice Cream. They round
the corner of the exit drive, hugging
the curb to forage asphalt. The drake
scans traffic on Broadway, unconcerned
about his distance from Lakeside Park.
He is drawn by syrup, sugar cone,
vanilla wafer. He stops,
pulls his yellow feet below his wings
and sits in the traffic lane. The hens follow,
assured by confidence, webbed poise
amid blaring horns, waffle crumbs,
strawberry yogurt spreading like snowmelt.

Root of the Forgotten

Night releases the earth slowly, retreating
Back into the rainspouts and the geranium pots.
It lays low at the root of the forgotten
Enveloping the blade of a hoe, a blue
Prescription bottle, the plastic
Shine of the slug's trace. Even
As we are pulled from our beds,
A foothold of darkness
Hollows the blankets,
Shies from memory, refuses
The light of day.

Peas from Carrots

You've become that old woman in the chair, forearm
Pressed to your chest like a shield, fingers curled,
Not in the readiness of a fist, but curved
Against the thumb, inert, like a potato on a fork.
Your damaged vision splits your supper,
Peas from carrots, butter from bread, chicken from bone.
You slur the story of your life into a series of inflexions
And whispers, half words and syllables
That slip between your lips like mixed vegetables.
Your family spoons through them privately
And pushes them to a corner of the plate, they are ready
In case one should spittle out onto your chin
And with the swipe of a towel
Be stroked into a thought.

Cat in the House

The night after they buried her mother
she crawled into bed and pulled the quilts
up to her neck, the light left on to read.
The cold slipped in behind her, between the wall
and her back. She had her book
broken at the spine, flattened
like sleep, the page
unturned. Death
milled around the house.
She could hear it jumping
from the counter to the floor, scratching
at the base of the door, overturning
bowls, jiggling spoons
left in cups.

Acknowledgements

Ann Arbor Review: "Auction of Small Ghosts", "Hiking Richland Creek", "Wild Life in the Big City"

Atticus Review: "Secrets"

Barnwood Poetry Magazine: "Beans from Apple Butter"

Blue Island Review: "Goldfish below Ice"

Big River Poetry Review: "Orion in the Sweet Gum"

Boston Literary Magazine: "Maslow's Hierarchy", "Passage to Saturn", "Tacitus Silent at Last"

The Buddhist Review: "Noble Silence"

The Buffalo Creek Review: "The Only Photograph of the Boy as a Child", "Walking through the Cemetery with a Three Year Old"

The Camel Saloon: "The Proper Fish", "Sunday Ducks", "Three Hundred"

Camroc Press Review: "Discovering Rose"

Caper Literary Journal: "A Mother's Omen", "Listening for Bees in the Floor of the Old School House"

The Dead Mule School of Southern Poetry: "Deep on Punt Return", "Hansel and Gretel Get the Word on the Street", "Playing Mafia Wars on Library Computers"

English Journal: "Papas First Trumpet"

Eunoia Review: "Bracket for Normal", "Bumper Sticker", "Poem for Sale", "Straining Tea", "Unlikely"

The Fat City Review: "Studied Traffic"

Flint Hills Review: "The Second Generation Visits Vietnam"

Foundling Review: "Great Blue Heron"

Front Porch Review: "Winter Dance"

Full of Crow Poetry: "Dear Badass"

Gutter Eloquence: "Biology Lab", "Neighbors Don't Understand"

A Handful of Stones: "Deep Wood Koan"

Heavy Feather Review: "Buddhists Call It Monkey Mind"

Hobo Camp Review: "Thomas Paints a Fence"

I-70 Review: "Renting a Chicken", "Waving Mustard in Surrender", "Winter Solstice"

Kansas Arts Association (KAC) Website: "Cinderella"

Kansas English: "Among Bees", "Brainwashing as Self-Help", "English Class Angler"

Long Island Quarterly: "Old Mr. Ramsey Recalls His Fear of Snakes"

The Mas Tequila Review: "Suicide Squeeze", "T-Ball on the Boulevard"

Mead: The Magazine of Literature and Libations: "Highway Signs Are Painted Green"

The Midwest Quarterly: "The New Arrangement"

New Letters: "Cat in the House", "Seventh Grade Communication Arts"

The New Mexico Poetry Review: "No Account Gordon"

New York Quarterly: "Peas from Carrots", "Root of the Forgotten"

Ofi Press Mexico (Mexico City): "Union", "The Velvet Revolution Reaches Kansas"

150 Poems for 150 Years: "Reading William Stafford in a Snowstorm"

The Orange Room Review: "Hitching by Night across New Mexico"

Poetry Bay: "Eliot Ness Pisses on Crime"

Prairie Schooner: "Farm Notes", "Kisser"

Pyrokinection: "Lorca Deep Fries a Turkey"

Quantum Poetry Magazine (New Zealand): "Touch"

The Quarterly: "After Johnny's Drug Overdose Wally Keeps His Memory Alive By Begging Cookies at Truck Stops", "Boys Dig Through the Neighbor's Trash Only to be Beset by Great Mystery"

Ramshackle Review: "Performing the High Wire", "The Gift"

Red River Poetry Review: "Applause for Widow Audubon", "Wally Steals Oscar"

ReThink Topeka: "Shoveling Snow at the High School", "Spinning Donuts with Grandfather in his Old Ford"

Rusty Truck: "Jesus Studies the Blueprints", "Teen Age Jesus"

Short, Fast and Deadly: "City Council Hires a Cannon", "Hawk on the Practice Field", "Henry's Romance"

Silent Things: "Merit Badge", "On Christmas Morning at Mother's You Wait in Line to Use the Bathroom"

SOFTBLOW: "Brothers", "Cataract Love Poem", "Digging Up the Septic Tank", "Michael Hogard's Wake"

Stone Highway Review: "Heat Wave"

Summerset Review: "Goldfish with the Faces of Old Men"

To the Stars through Difficulty: "Fletching"

Victorian Violet Press and Journal: "At-Risk in Bonehead English", "The Teacher Canoes through Seventh Hour"

Wilderness House Literary Review: "During Hard Times the Boat Maker Resorts to Football Helmet Repair", "Sometimes the End is a Beginning", "Subsistence Farming", "Tuning Her Guitar at the Safe House"

Wild Goose Poetry Review: "Animals We Kept", "Another Tornado Warning", "Legacy", "Soaring Fins"

Willows Wept Review: "Canoeing in Ice Storm", "A History of Leaves", "Tupperware"

The Yellow Ham: "The Professor Busts a Local Meth Lab", "While Taking Tickets at the Drive-In Theater, Wally Discovers the Cost of Chivalry"

Zeitgeist: "Pick-Up", "The Return"

Notes

"Change Comes to Cabbage" is an ekphrastic poem after a print by Doris Lee, entitled "Helicopter".

"Cinderella" was a winner in the Professional Poet Category, *Kansas Poetry Month Contest*, April 2010.

"English Class Angler" begins with a quote from Wendell Berry's poem, "The Plan".

"Farm Notes" also appeared in *Cooking Chili on the Day of the Dead*, Aldrich Press, 2013.

"Hansel and Gretel Get the Word on the Street" was selected as a poem of the day in Jason Ryberg's *Head Full of Boogeymen/Belly Full of Snakes (or Confessions of a Low Status American Male)* November 25, 2011.

"Performing the High Wire" appeared in the *Whirlybird Anthology of Kansas City Writers*.

"Reading William Stafford in a Snowstorm" appeared as a *Kansas Dailey Poem in Your Pocket*, Kansas Arts Commission in April 2011.

"Three Hundred" is after *Self-Immolations in Tibet*, www.savetibet.org, International Campaign for Tibet (ICT).

Thank You

The author wishes to thank the following friends and editors for their insights into this collection:

Matt Bolch, Wayne Bockelman, Tom Burns, Terry Collins, Dana Cope, Robert Day, Eileen Frank, Raymond Hammond, Michael Heffernan, Mike Hogard, J.T. Knoll, Dan Jaffe, Adam Jameson, John Laflen, Gordon Lish, Jo McDougall, Jerre Medford, Cory Ossana, Al Ortolani Sr., Trenton Stern,

and, of course, to my loving wife Sherri.

I would like to add a special thanks to Kwame Dawes, Robert Stewart, William Trowbridge, and George Wallace for their time spent with this manuscript, and to Jacque Allen Forsher for her cover art.

About the Author

photo by Sherri Ortolani

Al Ortolani was born in Huntington, New York in 1952. He was raised in Pittsburg, Kansas, attending Pittsburg State University where he received his B.S. in Education, M.A. in English and an Ed.S. in Higher Education. As a boy, he dreamed of playing second base for the New York Yankees. When the scouts failed to show, he began writing poetry. Ortolani is a career public school teacher in Kansas. His poetry and reviews have appeared in journals such as *Prairie Schooner, New Letters, The Midwest Quarterly, The English Journal,* and the *New York Quarterly.* He has four books of poetry, *The Last Hippie of Camp 50* and *Finding the Edge,* published by Woodley Press at Washburn University, *Wren's House,* published by Coal City Press in Lawrence, Kansas, and *Cooking Chili on the Day of the Dead* from Aldrich Press in California. He is on the Board of Directors of the Kansas City Writers Place and is an editor with *The Little Balkans Review.* He currently lives in the Kansas City area with his wife Sherri.

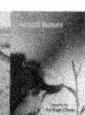